ROAD TRIP TO SUCCESS

CORY HERCHENROEDER

Roxanne,
Thank you for always being such a strong person. I love your family as if it was my own. I genuinely appreciate the love and support you've shown me over the years. I hope this book helps guide you through your upcoming "Road Trips".

Much love,
Cy H

Copyright © 2018 Cory Herchenroeder

All rights reserved.

ISBN:
ISBN-13:978-1724514714

DEDICATION

This book is dedicated to every person that has been told they weren't good enough, smart enough, or that they couldn't do something. Me publishing this book is proof that if you set your mind to doing something great, nothing can stop you.

CONTENTS

	FOREWORD	1
1	INTRODUCTION	4
2	WHAT IS YOUR EXCUSE?	8
3	HOW DO YOU DEFINE SUCCESS?	15
4	DOES ADVERSITY DEFINE YOU?	22
5	PREPARATION IS KEY	34
6	FIND YOUR WHY	48
7	FIND YOUR PASSION	59
8	VALUE	73
9	BUILD YOUR NETWORK	83
10	GOAL SETTING: ROAD TRIP METHOD	99
	ACKNOWLEDMENTS	114

FOREWORD

It's a summer afternoon in Springfield, Missouri. The sun is beating down. There's no cloud coverage and no wind. My know-it-all Iphone claims its 91 but, on the turf, it feels like 1000 degrees. My shirt is now a dark grey, soaked from all my sweat. Sweat is dripping down my face, blinding me and coating my lips with a saltiness I can't get rid of. I'm standing on the end line of the soccer field, utterly exhausted. No one is making me do this, in fact, few people even know that I'm out here. I begin to convince myself that no one would truly care if I stopped right now, went home to the air conditioning and called it a day. But see, that's the thing, when it's easy and you want to do something, motivation is easy to find. It's when everything is telling you no, it feels like you have a mountain on your back and that little voice in your head won't stop convincing you that you don't need it... that's when you dig. It's at times like these when your will to succeed has to outweigh your temptation to stay within your comfort zone. It's at those moments when the motivated are separated from the weak because they are able to grab onto something so deep inside that nothing will stand in their way. It's what makes the difference between accomplishing your dreams and watching someone else enjoy the success of the hard fought battle. What motivates each of us is different and we can't compare ourselves to others, you must search for what is meaningful for YOU. It may change throughout our lives and mold to our ever-changing personalities but challenging ourselves to constantly explore the depths of our dreams, fears and desires will allow us to use them to propel us to new heights. You may not be able to control what is happening around you, but you can ALWAYS control your fight!

ROAD TRIP TO SUCCESS

My whole life I've pushed myself based off proving others that doubt me (and myself at times) wrong. But today, when I look up from behind my sweat drenched face, I experience something different. I see a man who under no obligation is standing in front of me in the same agonizing heat, receiving no compensation, gaining no personal benefit. Few times in my life have I felt driven to push myself due to the unwavering belief someone has in me. But it's in the way he looks at me that I can tell he almost wants me to succeed as badly as I want to. His reassuring voice and enthusiastic demeanor speak louder than any language convincing me that I can do this. We both refuse to let me give up. I look up and see him, wanting nothing more than to make him proud. So, despite every muscle in my body begging me to stop, I take a breath, step up to the line and when he yells, "go", I sprint.

MUCH LOVE,
Mary Disidore
Missouri State University Women's Soccer
Class of 2018

-

Chapter 1

INTRODUCTION

Are you getting everything you want out of your life? Are you doing everything in your power to be successful or are you just living life going through the motions? My goal with this book is to help you move your life in a new direction. Whether that is starting you out on your road to success, or if you already see yourself as being successful and you're looking for new tools to gain momentum to push yourself even higher, then this book is for you.

Throughout 'Road Trip to Success', you will find real stories from my life that have gotten me to where I am today. Some stories, in the moment, were things that I thought were extreme negatives, others are stories that have propelled my career because I've found success in certain areas of my life. All of my stories, though, are ones that I had to learn from, and I hope that through my experiences you can find the lessons that I took away from them.

Who Am I?

I understand that a vast majority of the people that are reading this book have no idea who I am, and are probably asking, "What gives this guy the right to try to tell me how to be successful? What has he done?" My only answer to those questions would be that I'm a person that has gone through a lot of adversity, as people say, "the chips were stacked against me," but I found different values and different attributes within myself through my journey that have gotten me to where I am today. I am a strong believer in every person having their own 'path'. For example, my family and I all have very different paths; I have my Master's Degree in Education/Administration, my older brother has an Associate's Degree, my older sister started college, but had to leave school because she got pregnant with her son. I'm not including this to bash my siblings, quite the opposite actually. I am extremely proud of both my brother and sister, and the things that they have accomplished. My brother is happily married with a steady job, and he is living a life HE is happy with. My sister has dominated being a single mother to my amazing nephew, I could never begin to fathom how hard of a job that is and yet she works nonstop to make sure he has a life that she believes he'll be proud of.

I played soccer for 4 years in college away from home and I loved it. I loved it so much in fact, I made a career out of it. My first 2 years in coaching were at the same school that I played at which was a smaller NAIA school. Then, I had the amazing opportunity to go coach at a Division 1 school in the area for over 2 years, and since then I've moved on to a different Division 1 school even further from home. With all of that being said, it just goes to show that we all have our own road to what we consider success.

My job as a coach is to give my players the keys to success on a daily basis. I try to help them each find what inspires them, and continue to motivate them by using the values that I hope to teach you in this book. Hopefully we can figure out the things that are holding you back, we can define what success means to you, help you understand what true preparation is, find your WHY, determine what you are passionate about, define what YOUR value is, build your network, understand adversity, and finally implement all of those values into my goal setting method: Road Trip Method. Let this 'road trip' begin!!

Chapter 2

WHAT'S YOUR EXCUSE?

There is Always an Excuse

Excuses are something that we hear a lot when things aren't going our way. "I didn't have enough time." "I can't..." Everyone has an excuse for why they aren't in the place that they think they should be or why they aren't successful.

Identify your excuse and listen to yourself say the excuse. What is it in your life that is allowing you to say "No" or "I can't". Is it the little voices inside your head? Think about every time you've had to make a decision that had potential to be life altering, whether that was buying a new car, buying a house, applying for a job, or asking for that big promotion. Now ask yourself what excuse has kept you from pursuing those things? Is your excuse based on a fear? Do you not feel like you have time to accomplish your tasks at hand? Those are the two most common bases of excuses, FEAR and TIME.

Nullify Your FEAR

Fear plays a huge role when we make excuses. Do you allow the fear of what other people will think about your decision effect your final decision? Do you have a fear of putting yourself in an uncomfortable situation? Do you have a fear of doing something out of the ordinary or new?

Once you've identified your excuse as being a fear of something, you have to then make a choice; Do have what it takes to push yourself through the fear? Or, are you going to give up and continue on the path that you are already on? The choice here should be obvious. Is it easy to put yourself in a situation that you aren't comfortable in? Of course not! But, if you want to evolve then you have to be willing to take risks in your life, and this is a major step. I say this to my players all the time, "Learn to be comfortable, making yourself uncomfortable." The more often you throw yourself into uncomfortable positions, the less they seem uncomfortable.

Find TIME to be Successful

Time is something that no one can completely control, but it is something we can manage. When someone says, "There just aren't enough hours in the day…" the first question in my head is, "How are you prioritizing your time?" Obviously, there are only 24 hours in a day, the average person sleeps about 6-8 hours a night, so in those other 16 hours how can you be as productive as possible?

Being a college athlete, time management was something that I'd had a ton of practice with. Whether it was going to practices, going to class, traveling, working on homework, trying to find time to have a social life, games, etc. I believe being a college athlete helped me master the art of time management.

Once I began coaching at the first Division 1 school, those time management capabilities were tested on a daily basis. At this school, I was the assistant coach for both the men and women's programs, I was coaching at the local soccer club 3 nights a week, and doing upwards of 10-12 private lessons per week that would last around an hour each. The number one priority for me was obviously working for the university, then there became the issue of which team do I spend more time with, how do I give each team equal time when I'm being pulled in multiple directions, is this even possible? I have to tell you, there were many days that I questioned if I was doing the right thing.

My typical day consisted of doing office work from around 9:00am to about 1:00pm then from 1:00pm to around 6:00pm I'd be on our stadium field either doing private sessions, men's practice, or women's practice, and finally on Monday, Tuesday and Thursday I'd drive to the local club to coach from 6:30-8:30pm. In my mind at the time, those hours were long enough to try to give everyone equal attention. In reality, that would never be enough. I went on for about 6 months telling myself that I was doing enough, and I didn't have any more time to give to anyone. I was doing just enough to get by and I was, in turn, not happy with the results that I was getting back from my players, my projects, or my social life.

I continuously generated this thought process that "I don't have time", when in reality I was just being lazy. Yes, I worked 10-11 hour days pretty often, but I never really felt that I utilized my time efficiently. Once I decided that time was something that I could manage, I found a way to prioritize the more important aspects of my job. Within the 10-11 hours that I'd typically worked, I'd make more time for structured private sessions (formulate a weekly schedule), I'd come in earlier when need be to work on the office work that I'd typically do throughout the day. This would allow me to put more time into other aspects of each team (film sessions, individual player development meetings, etc.), and most importantly be more engaged in my players lives and getting to know them as people off of the field. I genuinely believe that the more time you put into getting to know someone, the harder that person will work for you, whether you're a college soccer coach, a manager at McDonald's or a CEO of a multi-billion dollar company.

Learning the skill of time management is not easy, but it is a vital component for anyone that hopes to be successful. One of the key moments of my story was when I realized that I had the opportunity to 'create' more time just by changing the things I held high on my priority list. Once I took a look in the mirror and paid attention to the things that were actually most important to me, it opened up more time and allowed me to focus more on the things that would put me in position to be successful.

Wrap-Up (What is Your Excuse?)

It is extremely important to understand that excuses are something that can't be a part of our lives. Every excuse that we make prolongs our success. If you aren't successful right now, take a look in the mirror and identify what your excuse is. Is the fear of something holding you back? If so, go out and do something outside of your norm until you get more comfortable, but don't allow the fear of the unknown hold you back from your successes. Are you struggling to find time to get everything done that you feel needs to be done? Start prioritizing your time by what is genuinely important to you, and determine what you think you need to be successful. Eliminate your excuses, and you will start to see successes.

Chapter 3

HOW DO YOU DEFINE SUCCESS?

What is Your Definition of Success?

Every person has their own interpretation of what the word 'success' means. Success can be linked to many things, such as, happiness, servant leadership, money, family, etc. When you are defining what success means to you, it is extremely important to relate success with what drives you.

Defining SUCCESS is no easy task, for a lot of us what we think of first when we hear the word success is getting the big promotion at work, landing the job that pays 6 figures, or winning championships. Your first priority when defining what success means to you, is to be EXTREMELY CLEAR as to what you are hoping to accomplish. If you are unclear as to what you are trying to get out of your life, you're going to be chasing EVERYTHING, and it will lead to NOTHING.

Once you've established a clear understanding of how you define success, establish the next steps in your life geared toward that motivating factor. An easy and common example of this would be if you're definition of success is earning a lot of money. If money is your motivating factor, then you need to establish different steps that allows compensation to be the forefront of your thought process. For example, if you're selling a product, what can you do to get your product in front of as many people as possible? If you're working in a commission based market, what are the steps you can take to reach the highest level of commission within your company?

There are many other examples you could use as your definition of success, but a big one for me is servant leadership. Servant leadership involves helping others perform at a higher level. To establish steps to become a successful servant leader you have to first realize who/what you are trying to reach. For example, is your goal to help the homeless, help people within your church, help those that are sick, help student-athletes realize their dreams, or help businessman/businesswomen become stronger in their lines of work? Now, what are you going to do to get in front of as many of those people as possible? Can you go to a convention that you know entrepreneurs will be attending? Would you be willing to host a public forum that was geared toward helping the homeless population in a certain area? Can you volunteer at your local hospitals to help give the sick a new outlook on life? You will always be able to find ways to make the answer to these questions a "Yes" if your success is riding on it.

Can Your Definition of Success Change?

Success, and your definition of success, should not be a concrete answer. Our everyday lives are ever-changing and always evolving, the same way our definitions of what make us successful should be.

At an early stage in life, a success could be getting an "A" in Chemistry, at another stage graduating from high school could be your next success, and then graduating college, getting a Master's Degree, landing your first job, becoming financially stable, getting married, having a family. The list could go on and on, but the purpose is to be aware of where you are in life, genuinely understand what you want in this period of your life, and what will propel you higher in the next stage.

Not only can the stage of your life dictate your definition of success, but so too can the individual project or goal you're currently working on. Throughout the extensive process of attaining a long-term goal, there could be many smaller successes along the way that could also equate to your overall success. Don't allow the length of long-term goals jade your optimism, find ways to have small successes along the journey.

Is Success Your Final Destination?

Now that we've talked about the different stages of life and what the true definition of success is, let's talk about what happens when we start becoming 'successful'. Accomplishing a goal, reaching that next stage in your life, and feeling confident in where you've come is a great thing, but the success of one goal is just the starting point of another. So many of us go through life and latch on to the 'success' that we have had, and we become content in knowing that is what has made us who we are. What we don't tend to realize is that there are so many small successes that we completely overlook that could help shape and define who we are, to help us evolve as we go in to the next stages of our lives. By overlooking those small successes and really focusing on that one success, we become content. Being content stifles evolution and prevents you from reaching your true and full potential. We should always allow each success, no matter how big or small, to be a stepping stone for your next great journey.

In your heart, you should always believe that you are meant to be greater than the person that you are today. No matter where you are in your career, or in your life, you've gone through a lot to get to where you are right now, but THIS, RIGHT NOW is not the end point. Today is the day that you recognize your successes and prepare yourself to be a greater success in the future.

Wrap-Up (How Do You Define Success)

There are many different interpretations of what the word 'success' means. The only thing that should matter to you is what YOUR definition of success is. Be extremely clear about how you define success. Don't allow your definition to be a 'concrete' answer, allow your definition of success to adjust and adapt with the different stages of your life, and the different adjustments and adaptations you'll have to make. One success should never be your final destination. Always believe that you are meant to be greater than you are today. A single success can be the destination for one journey, but also the first step to your next.

Chapter 4

DOES ADVERSITY DEFINE YOU?

Turn a Negative Circumstance into A Positive Mindset

Do you have the ability to turn a negative

circumstance into a positive mindset? If you can't, then you will not have a 100% success rate in your life, you will fail. Through your failures you will learn that you can only control the control-ables. Adversity is something that we all have to live with, and be able to adapt to.

Imagine coming home from school one day as a 17-year old kid to see your dad (who you don't live with), and your sister sitting in your living room with blank stares on their face. From the moment you walk into the room you know something isn't right. You look at both of them and ask, "What's going on?" Neither of them can respond right away, they both look at each other with tears forming in their eyes, when finally, your dad says, "You need to sit down please." At this point, as a 17-year old, millions of thoughts are running through your head thinking about all of the things that you've done in the past few weeks that you could possibly be in trouble for. As I finally sit down in the computer chair on the far side of the room, my brother walks into the room at the same time, and my dad tells him to have a seat next to him on the couch. The next moment changed my life forever. "Your mother passed away this morning..." Honestly, my dad talked for about 3 minutes after that statement, and I couldn't hear a word of what he said. In that moment, my chest felt like a 1000-pound weight just fell on top of it. All I could think about is how can I possibly live without her?

Growing up we are always asked, "Who is your hero?" "Who inspires you?" Those were, and still are, the easiest questions for me to answer. My mom was my best friend, who I have always been inspired by, and who will always be my hero. I always had this natural desire to make her proud of me, I guess that is mostly the case for any child to want their parent to be proud of them, but with my mom it always seemed like if I didn't accomplish what I set out to do I was failing her. I always told her I was going to graduate from college, be a professional soccer player, and never make my family live paycheck to paycheck. When she was diagnosed with cancer, her and I spent less and less time together because of her long hospital stays, but the time that we did spend together, there was never a silent moment. She'd tell me all the things that she wished she'd done in her life, we'd talk about the life she wanted me to have, and every single time we saw each other she'd tell me, "No matter what you do in life, know that I'm already proud of the person you are."

The day that my dad had to tell me the hardest news of my life, the first thing I did was ask if I could go play soccer. Soccer has always been an outlet for me. It's always been what has simplified everything else in my life. When I'm on the soccer field, I can forget everything else that is going on in my life, it has allowed me to keep my sanity. This day though, 6 of my friends were already at the soccer field that we'd always go to. My dad hesitantly dropped me off at the field to be with my friends because, up to this point, I hadn't really shown much emotion to the news of my mother passing and I don't think he knew what else to do for me. I get to the field, and for whatever reason, I thought my friends had already known what was going on, and I took one step on to the field with them, saw their faces and immediately dropped to my knees sobbing. I vividly remember my best friend, Pete Smith, picking me up off the field and walking me to the benches asking me what was going on. My response wasn't that my mom passed away, it was "You already know.." Of course none of them had any idea, so after a few more times of them asking me I finally choked out what had happened. As I finally got the story out, all of my friends told me we probably should just leave, but that was the last thing I could have ever wanted. We stuck around for a little over an hour, and played a couple of games just shooting the ball at the goal. There was a moment that I just looked up to the sky, saw the clouds passing by, and thought to myself "this is where I'm supposed to be."

As I said, when my mom was alive I lived to make her proud of me. Now that she's passed, with everything I do, I continue to have that same mindset, "Would my mom be proud of the person I'm becoming?" Obviously, there are moments in life that all of us would love to go back to and do differently; however, having the ability to ask myself that question time and time again with the answer consistently being "Yes", has given me a positive perspective on this terrible situation.

This situation was obviously one of the worst things that I've had happen to me in my lifetime. That was a very dark time in my life, I remember my mom's funeral like it was yesterday. Hundreds of people were gathered to see her, I sat there watching everyone go up and down the aisle to see her, and all I could think about was how many people she touched with her life. I didn't want the memory of my mom to be something sad, I wanted to continue her legacy as something positive, and that is why I try to use her as one of my greatest motivating factors.

Everyone goes through different types of adversity. We all have our dark moments, but not all of us have the ability to make those moments a motivating factor. This is not something you can just snap your fingers and BOOM, now it's there. It is very much a practice of mental toughness, and something you have to continuously keep reminding yourself of. If you allow your negative moments define you, you will never grow and evolve as a professional, or as a person in general.

You WILL Fail

There are a lot of people that see failure as the end of the road. I like to think of failure as the beginning of your next great opportunity. Your character will be built not by your failures, or even the number of times that you fail, but by how you REACT, ADAPT, and EVOLVE after each of those failures. Each of your failures is just teaching you one more way of how not to do something.

Through many different failures, you will find experiences that will give you the opportunity to decide whether you want to learn from them or not. When you choose to learn from your failures you will begin to see your successes come more frequently. If you choose to keep doing the same things and continue to fail over and over, that is the definition of insanity, and the result will not change.

Control the Control-ables

As we go through life, we try to find successes through so many different avenues that when we fail, we don't always understand why. Most often, when we fail and we don't understand why it is something that is completely out of our control, and that is very hard for some people to comprehend. As you are 'building your empire', you get so invested in what you are doing that you think you can control everything, which is simply not the case. You will never be able to control if someone shows up on time or not. You will never be able to control if there is a technical issue as you are about to give a presentation. You will never be able to control the number of people that attend your show, camp, presentation, etc.

Every aspect of your life will be judged by other people you are in contact with whether you like it, want it, realize it or not. If you allow those judgments to impact your life in a negative light, you have indeed failed. However, it is okay to reflect on the judgments of others, but at the end of the day you have to stick to the path that you've chosen because that is what your passion dictates. Unfortunately, you will NEVER be able to control the things that people are saying about you, your progress, or the path that you are on. There WILL be judgments; it is your job to stay focused on the task at hand, and remember the reasons you started down this path.

Manipulate your focus to the things that you can control that will make you a success. Understand you need to control how you connect with people. Learn to connect with every person you speak with. Believe that every person you meet could be the person that changes your life forever.

Having the ability to put yourself in someone else's

shoes is a skill that's used in a lot of sales training, but can be used in nearly everything you do in your life. When I was selling insurance, one of the reasons I was so successful was because of my ability to put myself in my client's shoes. I can empathize with most people when they have a problem, and being able to understand, and genuinely wanting to help my client, put me above other salesman at my company. I went into every phone call thinking that today could be the worst day of this person's life so what can I do to be the bright light to their dark day? This attitude led to my clients trusting me.

Control your leadership skills at all times, as you will always have people looking at the examples you set. Always be approachable; Allow your co-workers, employees, colleagues, etc. see that you care about them; be a great mentor. People will always want to work with/for you if they know they can count on you, because they will want to return the favor. Always keep an open and honest line of communication. Never let there be a question as to what you want or need out of someone. Without great communication, there will be questions. With questions come insecurity in your employee's ability to do their job, which in turn, means your business won't be as successful as it could be.

How hard you work is something that should never be in question, you have the ability to always control your WORK RATE. Always be the one to set the example of what the work rate of your business should look like. It doesn't matter whether you are running a business or coaching a team, if the leader is working as hard as they can, everyone will be more apt to follow in the same fashion. As an example, say you have 30 people in your business (or on your team), and 27 people are dominating productivity and working extremely hard, those 3 people that aren't pulling their weight are going to be extremely apparent. Now, those 3 people have to ask themselves a question, "Is this where I'm supposed to be?" More often than not, the answer to that question is going to be 'no'.

When people are trying to reach success, there are times when their MORAL VALUES will be called in to question. These moral values are something that you can always control. Have integrity in everything you do. When you have earned the trust of people around you, they will want to promote you and the things that you are trying to build. As you are 'building your empire', never cut corners because it is the easy thing to do. Having the ability to do the right thing, even if it happens to be the hard option, the option that will take more time, or even the option that isn't the most popular may not be something that will win over the people you're with in the moment, but they will respect you more for making those decisions in the long run. Take the time to put in the work that is necessary to have a successful brand. I was listening to a podcast recently and the guest speaker said, "If you walked into a coffee shop, would you be okay with the barista filling your cup up ¾ of the way full?" Absolutely not!!

Wrap-Up (Does Adversity Define You?)

Having the ability to turn a negative circumstance into a positive mindset is something that is extremely difficult, but in my mind, it is essential to allowing yourself to be successful. Understand that YOU WILL

FAIL, it's a given, but your character will be built, not by your failures or number of times that you fail, but by how you REACT, ADAPT, and EVOLVE after each of those failures. Learn that you can only control the things that you can control. There is no point in putting stock into the bits of adversity that you can't control, accept the failure, analyze the things that you can control from the situation, and learn from it for next time. Make yourself less apt to fail by controlling how you connect with the people around you, your leadership skills, your work rate, and your moral value.

Chapter 5

PREPARATION IS KEY

Formulate a Routine

How could having a routine possibly impact my day? In my eyes, having a routine is one of the most underrated values of them all. Some people take routine to the next level, which is being superstitious about things

(I am one of those people), but having the ability to create a routine that allows you to prepare yourself for each day is extremely important. That routine could be something as simple as when you wake up in the morning you have to turn on the coffee pot, get in the shower, brush your teeth, make your breakfast and then write down the tasks that you want to complete for the day. Every day your routine takes you through that same cycle, now at the beginning of each day you've hand written all of the tasks that you need to complete that day which, first, will help you remember what you need to do throughout the day, and second, if you forget, you have something to reference back to.

My typical routine is pretty similar to that of what I just referenced (except I don't make my own coffee). First thing I do when I wake up is shower, then brush my teeth, then I will write down the tasks that I need to complete that day, sometimes when I know I won't be carrying my backpack with my notepad in it around all day, I will write my top priority tasks on my left hand I write them on my left hand because I wear my watch on my left wrist and I look at my watch literally every five minutes (I can't help it), so it is a constant reminder of the different tasks I need to complete. Once I finish writing down my tasks, the last thing that I always do before I leave my house every morning is say OUT LOUD, "Be better today than you were yesterday, so new doors will open for you tomorrow." I honestly have no idea when I started saying that, where I heard it from, or for that matter, if I'd ever heard anyone ever do that. I use that sentence to get me motivated every single day because I know if I can work hard today, I will be better than I was the day prior, which will mean tomorrow, I will be in a better position to further my career.

It is so important to have the ability to self-reflect and self-analyze each day, and having a routine that jumpstarts that is key. Understand that having a routine does not make you weird or superstitious, it allows you to prepare yourself to be successful.

Always Be the Most Prepared Person in the Room

I'm sure everyone reading this book has heard the phrase "Preparation is Key". Well, I'm here to tell you whoever said that is absolutely correct. There are different levels of 'preparation' though. First, you have the 'minimum preparation', which is when you are doing just enough to get by, and when questions start to get asked, you really don't have any answers. Then, you have the 'mandatory preparation', which is when you do all the preparation you know that you need to get done for all of the basics of the project that you're working on. More than likely you can answer questions if you had to, but in all reality, you're the one that is hoping that none get asked. Finally, you have 'excessive preparation', which is when you have the answers to questions that people didn't even know to ask until you brought it up.

There are a lot of people in this world that say some successes are because someone got "LUCKY". There is no such thing as luck. Luck is the moment when all of your hard work and preparation comes to fruition. To put it in to sports terms, people have come up to me after games and said, "You guys were catching all the breaks tonight!" Well, yeah, of course we were. We were more prepared and executed our game plan. It's the same philosophy in the business world, people say, "Man, you are an overnight success story!" False! Starting a business doesn't just happen overnight, maybe their business hasn't been around long, but I can guarantee the time, preparation, trials and tribulations to find a formula that worked was nothing that could be done 'overnight'.

What is Your Backup?

A huge part of being prepared is always having a solid backup plan. If you are going to be putting tons of your own time and effort into a project, don't let anything stand in the way of you completing it. To be fully prepared, planning for any and all setbacks is key.

At this point in my career as a college soccer coach, I've learned that I will always need something in my 'back pocket' just in case something goes wrong. This particular story is about a girl that I was in the process of recruiting to my second Division 1 school. This girl was our number 2 recruit for her recruiting class on our recruiting board (a recruiting board is where coaches on staff will rank their recruits as to which will take priority over others, or may be worth more scholarship money, etc.). Usually, coaching at the level that I was at, mid major, our number 1 and 2 recruits would most likely try to go to a school in a higher conference and/or bigger school. This girl was extremely interested in our program and what we were trying to build. She came on a visit to our campus and I gave her, her parents and a couple of her teammates a tour. After the tour, the other coaches on staff and I sat down with her and her family to talk about how we see her fitting into our program and answered any questions that she had. This girl is an extremely intelligent person, so she had a ton of questions for us. Typically, if a player is asking multiple questions that shows their interest level is high. Obviously, with this girl being very high on our recruiting board, asking a ton of questions, and just overall having what seemed to be a great day, we were excited!

As the meeting concluded, we offered her a substantial

amount of scholarship to come play for us. She was extremely thankful and told us that she wanted to go home and evaluate everything with her family before making her final decision. Of course, we were absolutely okay with that, and told her within 30 days she needed to update us as to where she was at in her process. As time went on, our staff was doing a phenomenal job of completing that particular recruiting class with the remaining amount of scholarship money that we had (this class was turning in to something pretty special), and this girl would be the cherry on top.

At this point, I had to make a decision. We were 'finished' with this recruiting class, assuming this girl decided to commit to us. So, do I stop looking for players in this class and shift my focus primarily to the next class? I just couldn't bring myself to do that. In my mind, if for whatever reason this girl decided to choose a different school over us, we would have a HUGE hole in the class that we just worked so hard to complete. I decided to come up with a backup plan, and then a third option, if for whatever reason that backup plan did not work. I got in contact with a coach that I knew well and explained our situation to him, and it just so happened that he had 4-5 players that I could choose from if I needed to. As it happened, two of the players that he recommended to me I believed were excellent fits for what we were looking for. As I'm giving my recruiting speech to these two girls, I fill them both in on the situation at hand, and both agree to wait 60 days to see what happens with the original recruit. Now, I feel solidified.

Being patient is not a trait that I was blessed with. Patience is something that I am continually working on to better myself. On the other hand, I also think my lack of patience is one of my positive characteristics, because I will never just wait around for an answer. If I don't have the answer to my first question, my mind will go straight to what the potential second and third questions may be, and start working on finding the answers to those questions while I'm waiting for the answer to my first question.

Going back to my story, having the two girls confirm that they were willing to wait 60 days for our first girl to make her decision made me feel solidified because I felt like I had ALL of my bases covered. I didn't feel like I could be left in a bad place (unless all three girls ended up telling me no). There always has to be that little bit of skepticism in your mind asking "What if?" Because if you aren't asking yourself about that question, there's no way that you can be prepared for it.

Be a Sponge

When you're in an environment that you're working with others, part of your preparation should be to be willing to learn from those around you. It doesn't always have to be you asking questions to others to learn. Many times it can be just watching or listening to the things they are doing or saying, I call that BEING A SPONGE.

My first job after finishing my Bachelor's Degree was selling insurance in an inbound call center. Obviously, growing up I'd heard all of the stereotypes about how salesmen are scumbags, especially insurance salesmen. After I made the decision to move to the Philadelphia area to sell insurance I was asked over and over again, "Why?" Honestly, I didn't have a great answer, the truth is,

I only moved there to be with my girlfriend at the time, and that was one of the only job offers I received (out of 89 applications). Little did I know, this job would have a major impact on my life.

When I started at this company, I had legitimately no knowledge of how to be a salesman or any knowledge of insurance for that matter. Luckily though, this company had a paid, 3-month training program that helped me prepare for my insurance licensing exam and also sales training. The entire first month, my 40-hour week was consumed with studying this book, hundreds of pages long, that went over all of the ins-and-outs of auto and homeowner's insurance (that was a brutal month). At the end of that first month, the company paid for me to go take my licensing exam, if I pass I move on to the sales training, if I failed I would only have one more opportunity to take the exam (you have to pay for your 2nd exam if you failed), and if I failed the second time then I would be fired. Knowing those were my options, I worked as hard as I could to pass this licensing exam on the first attempt, not so much because I thought I'd look bad if I failed the first time, but because I genuinely didn't know if I could afford to pay for the exam out of my own pocket.

Eventually, through the long days of studying, and taking that book home to study more every evening, I ended up passing on the first attempt. I was PUMPED! Now, I got to move on to sales training. The sales training was basically a 2-month training program where I learned the 'script'. I learned different techniques of how to approach customers and how to overcome objections, etc. There were 12 people in my 'class', so we'd always work on things in partners and groups. As we got more and more in depth with the training, you could see a few of us were doing better than others. After 6 weeks in sales training, myself and 3 others graduated early and get moved to 'THE FLOOR'. The floor is where all of the agents were receiving inbound customer calls, it was rows and rows and rows of agents. As you walk onto the floor, all you hear is the voices of hundreds of different people going through their script, overcoming objections, some loud-some soft. As you look at the floor, you see 15-20 rows of people with 10-15 agents in each row. Random flags sporadically placed along the top of random agents' cubicles were up and down each row. Every flag you see represents a sale that agent had for that day. To me, that was a bragging right, and I was all about that.

Now that we've graduated the 'academy', we've been placed on to a team (each different row is their own team). Everyone in each row was extremely close to one another, so everything I said on the phone could be heard by most people around me so, obviously, I could also hear what they said. It just so happened that I got put on a team with a few of the better sales people in our branch, and I wanted to take advantage of their experience. I found out very early being on the sales floor, that I wasn't good at sitting down while I spoke on the phone. I would pace around while going through the process, as I paced, I would do my best to listen to the things the other agents on my team would say. I would listen to HOW they were overcoming objections and began to understand how they would empathize with their customers, etc. On my desk, I had two different notepads, one notepad was to take notes on what the customer I was talking to was saying, the second was for when I heard something one of the other agents would say. When I heard something I liked, something I didn't understand or even something I laughed at because I couldn't believe they'd actually say that to a customer (it actually happened often) I'd write it down so I could ask them about it later. Like I said, before this job I'd had no sales experience at all so I was just trying to take everything in and build my own repertoire of sales techniques, just soaking everything up like a SPONGE.

When I wasn't on the phones, my boss allowed us to sit with other agents on our team to listen in on their calls. I'll be honest, I didn't understand at first why we did this, but I noticed that the people that genuinely took this seriously were the most successful, and the people that just used this time as a 'break' didn't last long in the business. Being able to be a sponge and soak up techniques, different ways to say things, inflections in your voice, etc. is fantastic, but the next step for me was the most important – deciding what information that I soaked up I could utilize in my pitches, and which information didn't really fit my personality or the way I go about my pitches. At the end of the day, if you're trying to be someone you aren't, people will see right through you, but if you're adding things to your pitch that reemphasize and strengthen your techniques, you're going to be more successful because of it.

The willingness to prepare yourself with the techniques of others is a difficult process to allow yourself to do. A lot of us think we know the perfect techniques or the perfect way to sell, and we just want to keep utilizing the techniques that we have already seen success with. Being open-minded and humble enough to implement someone else's techniques and evolve the system that you have created, will allow you to continue to grow and excel while other's stay stagnant.

Wrap-Up (Preparation is Key)

Working hard to be excessively prepared will always be time well spent. Have a routine that allows you to recognize and accomplish your goals each and every day. Don't let anyone in your position be more prepared than you. Have the answers to questions that haven't been asked, and always plan for setbacks. In your preparation, stay humble, don't hesitate to use techniques and strategies you've heard or seen used by your peers or colleagues.

Chapter 6

FIND YOUR WHY

Knowing your WHY is one of the most important values you can have as a person. At one point in my college coaching career there was a girl I was recruiting to come to my school, and the first time I saw her I was blown away. She was athletic, had a ton of skill, and seemed super confident in every aspect of her game. I reached out to her to let her know that I thought she did well and that I was interested in getting her to come to visit our campus and talk more about her coming to my school. Everything worked out well, she came to campus, loved it, and at the end of her visit our coaching staff told her that we wanted to continue to watch her development over the next 6 months before we decide on a scholarship offer. About a month later, myself and our other assistant went to watch her play again and she played okay, but wasn't someone that we rated highest on the field. In our minds we knew that 'Everyone has bad days, especially when they feel the pressure of college coaches watching them specifically.' In the next 3 months we had the opportunity to watch the girl play in 4 separate tournaments. She progressively showed less and less confidence in herself as each tournament went by until, while at the last tournament, she only played a total of 10 minutes in her final game.

After the final tournament, this girl called me and asked for my feedback (which is pretty common). Typically, I deflect the question and ask how they thought they played, or what were some things they did well, and things they could work on going forward, but with this girl (because I've seen her play so many times now) when I asked her those questions and she answered, I could tell they were rehearsed answers and she was genuinely upset, so I asked one additional question. WHY are you playing this game? Her response – "The last few months I've had such little confidence in myself, I can't give you a reason that I'm going to training every day. I don't enjoy going to play with the team I'm on, I hate being yelled at consistently by my coach, and I just never feel like what I'm doing is good enough. So, I feel like I've just been going through the motions lately." In this moment, I knew this girl was lost and I genuinely felt I had to help her, not just because I was a college soccer coach in the process of recruiting her, but because I hated hearing how this girl lost her way playing the game that she once loved.

Once I realized how low of a place she was in, I completely changed the subject off of me recruiting her to just talking about her as a person. I asked her things like, 'What do you want to accomplish in your life?' 'Who is the person in your life that you want to make the most proud in the things you want to accomplish?' 'What are the things in your life that you can't be without?' As we went on, you could tell her voice got a bit more upbeat talking about the different passions and values in her life that were important. Her answers were all vague for the most part, so I gave her a "Homework Assignment" that only she was going to know about, I was never going to ask her to read it to me or anyone else, but her task was to write down as many things in her life that were important to her. Then, try to narrow that list down to 7-10 different things that she felt were top priorities in her life. Finally, find a way to relate those priorities to what you want to get out of the next 5-7 years of your life, whether that is the atmosphere while you're playing soccer, deciding on a college to attend, what major you want to go in to, or even how to interact with your loved ones and/or friends.

In my career, I've had the unbelievable opportunity to have recruiting conversations with hundreds of players, but to this day, the conversation with this girl was the most important of them all. I've been in that LOST mode, and having to find a way out of that by yourself is extremely difficult, nearly impossible. Knowing that I've potentially helped this girl find her path is a happiness that I will never be able to put in to words.

What is Your Mission?

Have you ever thought to yourself, "What am I doing?" or "Is this really what I want to do with my life?" Those questions typically mean one of two things, you are confused on what you want in life or you are looking for a change. Start to make sense of what you are looking to get out of your life and formulate a mission statement.

Finding your mission is not something that will just

come to you overnight, it is a process, and it is ever-changing. This mission is something that you will mold your life around. There are many ways you can go about formulating your mission, but this is what worked for me. Allow yourself time to put your mission together ON PAPER. Literally lock yourself in a room away from any and all distractions. Give yourself a timeline. I gave myself a four-hour timeline, I've heard of other people taking a weekend away by themselves to think and reflect. The amount of time doesn't matter, just focus on the process. In this time, start listing literally everything that comes to mind that you genuinely believe is IMPORTANT in your life. As you complete your list of things that are important to you, start prioritizing them. My 'ranking system' was basically the top of this list were things I couldn't live without, down to things that were still important to me, but not necessities. As your priorities are coming in to place, you will see your core values really starting to line up. As you've finished prioritizing your list, you will most likely have a top-3 or potentially top-5 that you feel are 'must have's' in your life. This is extremely common, and to have the ability to sift through these and only genuinely focus on just 1 or 2 at a time is extremely unique. An example, as I finished prioritizing my list the top 5 were as follows:

- Family/Friends
- Servant Leadership
- Competition
- Soccer
- Sales

The next step now that you've broken down your list, whether you have narrowed it down to your top-5 or top-3, start to define each of the values in your list as to why they are important to you and also how this will impact your career. It is EXTREMELY important to break each of these down to as basic of principles as possible to make sure you are as clear as you can be on your final mission!

Family/Friends: Within my career, sometimes being near my family is not practical, but I still want to have the ability to go to any big moments in my family or close friend's lives (ie. Weddings, birthdays, birth of children, etc.). With my career taking me away from friends and family, I want my workplace environment to be that of a family. We all love each other, genuinely enjoy being around one another, sometimes we may not agree on things, but at the end of the day, we are in the trenches together willing to do whatever it takes for one another.

Servant Leadership: I want to have the opportunity to help people grow and motivate them to be successful. I am happiest when I know I've given my all for someone else, and I can see their growth and development as a person, student, and/or athlete.

Competition: Having the opportunity to compete every day will allow me to stay engaged and want to continuously improve myself. If I am doing the same thing day in and day out I will lose interest. Allowing my competitive nature to take control, will push me to reach my fullest potential.

Soccer: Having this sport in my life has given me the opportunity to go to college, learn countless life lessons, and have an outlet for when my life has reached deep valleys emotionally. Having the opportunity to teach, learn, and continue to grow the game is an extreme passion of mine.

Sales: For me, sales and sell is all about being able to connect with people from all different walks of life. For my career, being able to connect with people and try to sell them on a school, a specific team, or even the environment we've created within a team is always a great challenge, but those abilities to sell a product that I care deeply about are something I will continue to evolve and be better at.

Now I've completely broken down my list that I view as most important to me. Luckily for me, I am in a career where I have the ability to manipulate and adjust my workplace where I've actually included my top-5 values in to my career and in my everyday life. As a NCAA Division 1 SOCCER coach, I can continuously learn, teach and evolve the game that I am passionate about. While being a part of building this program, I go to many recruiting events in search of new players that I can SELL my program, our university, and the environment within our team to. Every week I spend nearly 60 hours with my team, whether that is the other coaches on staff, our athletic trainer, or our players I am a part of a FAMILY that I know will have my back if I ever need anything, as they know I will always have theirs. Every day our team trains at an extremely high level which allows us to COMPETE every weekend for a conference championship. Finally, being a college soccer coach allows me to LEAD young women to not only grow and develop as athletes, but also to help them become well-rounded people.

What Will Change When You Know Your WHY?

Now that you know your WHY, you may realize that what you've been doing doesn't fit your values. After you establish the things that are most important to you, you may start to rethink the career path that you are currently on. If that is the case, sit down and see if there are other career paths that fit what you are looking for. Some people may say that they are too old to change careers at this stage in their lives. That's a fair point, but are you doing what could make you genuinely happy going in to work every day? Are you successful doing it? Is your passion for the work that you are putting in what gets you through each day? If you answer no to any of those questions, then maybe the reason you're asking all of these questions is because you want something to change, no matter your age or financial situation.

How does your WHY impact those around you? All of the people that you surround yourself with will see that you are now living and working with a purpose. When you are doing things for a purpose, things will be easier for your coworkers because they are no longer having to carry a heavier burden, and they will respect your desire and passion.

Wrap-Up (Find Your WHY)

When you find your WHY, you will understand your PURPOSE. What is your mission? Write down your list of priorities so you can understand within yourself what is important and what will motivate you. Define each of your top-5 priorities, explain why each is important, and why it is a motivating factor for you. Once you figure out your WHY, the people around you will see a change in your work habits, the energy you bring to projects, and that is all because you will now be working with a purpose. There are times that you recognize, after you find your WHY, that you are not in the career field that fits your priorities. At this point, you may be thinking 'Have I put too much time into this career already?' 'I don't have the money to go back to school to get a new degree.' 'Is it worth it?'. To me, those are all excuses. Find a way to make it happen! Live the life you were meant to live!

Chapter 7

FIND YOUR PASSION

What Does It Mean to Be Passionate?

Passion. This is a word that gets thrown around a lot. What does it mean to actually be PASSIONATE about something? When you find certain things in your life that you're passionate about, you begin to realize those are the things that you genuinely don't want to live without, they become a necessity. You have found your passion when you can go into work every day and genuinely love what you are doing. When you have the willingness to get into the trenches and really grind for something because you believe in what it is that you are doing, that is passion. Most times you are not seeing the fruits of your labor right away, but being passionate means you are okay with the DELAYED GRATIFICATION. Now you know what you're working on has real meaning. When you understand your passions, you can start to prioritize your life.

The misconception of passion is having a strong emotion for something; however, you are most likely only enjoying it in the moment and eventually that infatuation fades over time. In life, we encounter many different things that give us INSTANT GRATIFICATION. We believe that because we are happy in this moment, we could do this thing, whatever it may be, for the rest of our lives. Having short term success in something gives you instant gratification, but as time wears on and you're grinding in the trenches, do you still have the same drive to better yourself? A majority of people live for the moments that give us that immediate desire, but they hate doing all of the hard work to sustain that same success. More often than not, things that give us that instant gratification will not bear the same amount of happiness as time goes on. Different things like success in a certain job, going to a destination vacation, or meeting a new person for the first time will give you that instant gratification, but as time goes on, and you learn new things, you may not have the same feelings.

Having the ability to differentiate our PASSIONS and our LUST is an extremely difficult practice. Passion will come with time, lust is the instant gratification. Sometimes the things that we're passionate about push us to limits that we never thought we'd have to encounter. When you know in your heart that you're going through all of that angst and sometimes pain, all the while you still have the drive to succeed, that is something you find passion in.

How Can You Find Your Passion?

As a kid, you are super passionate about so many things, such as, playing sports, riding bikes with your friends, reading books, etc., but as you get older you realize you want more things so you start grinding, finding different ways to earn money. The moment that those two paths cross and you find yourself grinding doing something you are passionate about, it's no longer a job, it's a lifestyle. You won't always find what you're passionate about on your first go around, it may take multiple failed experiences to realize what your true passion is.

Can You Pursue Multiple Passions?

I don't believe that passion is a singular value. I believe that passion ties in to your WHY and your belief system, so you are bound to have multiple passions.

As we've said, it takes a lot to really understand what you are passionate about. I've lived most of my life not really truly understanding the things that I'm passionate about. I've always had a general idea of the things that made me happy or things that I wanted to continue to do in my life, but until I sat down and really thought about the things I was passionate about it didn't hit me that I was in my ideal career. As I formulated my list of the values that I was genuinely passionate about my top 3 passions became extremely clear, servant leadership, competition, and soccer.

My definition of what I believe servant leadership means is having the willingness and the drive to put others' successes before your own. Having the opportunity to impact another person's life in a positive way is something that will always mean a great deal to me. In my career, I have the honor of coaching around 30 young women a year. Most of you will think to yourself, "As a soccer coach, all he does is teach the X's and the O's and tries to win games." Well, that is definitely a part of it, but that is the most minute part of my job. Making sure my girls are on the path to success in the classroom, giving them advice on how to handle certain life situations (ie. Boyfriend issues, family problems, or something as simple as being the person they feel comfortable enough to come to when they need to vent), arranging community service projects, and being a reference for their first career job are all things, plus many more, that I value a great deal within my career as a college soccer coach.

Competition has always been a driving factor in my life. Whether it was playing multiple different sports growing up, trying to beat my brother in video games, being a top sales agent in the country, or coaching at one of the highest levels I have always been drawn to success through competition. I am a firm believer that if you are not pushing yourself to compete with the highest level of competition, you're no longer evolving as a person. I will always push myself harder if I know I'm working hard for something bigger than myself, competing has ALWAYS been that something. I tell myself, my players, my friends, anyone that I talk to on a consistent basis, "I'm not okay with being average." Average people are okay with going through life and just getting by, elite people are willing to put in the blood, sweat, and tears it takes to compete with yourself, and anyone else trying to stand in the way of your success.

Soccer is my third passion. It's funny, I've been asked by multiple people, "How is SOCCER something that you are genuinely passionate about? That seems like more of a hobby." To most people, I'd say the sport you play growing up in pee-wee's, AAU, Little League, club, or even getting into high school and college is definitely just a hobby. The sport of soccer helped mold me in to the person that I am today. Through soccer I've learned teamwork, sportsmanship, determination, how to overcome adversity, resiliency, time management, and the list could go on. Soccer was my outlet after my mom passed away, and if I didn't have that to turn to who knows what my other options could have been in those dark times. For me, I know soccer is not just a hobby. I've given up being around my family, my friends, my hometown all because I want to share the passion that I have for this sport, and I want to give someone else the opportunity to find their outlet in their time of need.

I have definitely had my fair share of adversity in my life, but I've also had a TON of great things happen to me that I'm monumentally grateful for. One of my most life-altering moments was when I was offered my first college soccer coaching job at William Woods University. This was a blessing for multiple reasons because William Woods University was the school that gave me the opportunity to play college soccer, and now, they were the first school to allow me to coach. Having the ability to coach college soccer has allowed me to find a career that I can exercise my 3 greatest passions. I have the ability to help young women reach their greatest potential on the soccer field, as well as a person, and life in general. While my players are going through the long, grueling process of reaching their potential they are competing at an extremely high level each and every day in the classroom and on the field playing the sport that they love.

Having multiple things that you are passionate about is extremely common. A lot of people find themselves being passionate about family, friends, faith, and their careers. Having the ability to prioritize your passions will always be a difficult task. There will be different moments in your life that will call for the priorities in your life to adjust.

Allow People to See Your Passion

One of the greatest things about being passionate about something is allowing other people to see it. So many times in life we think about how it may or may not be 'cool' to get excited about certain things. Let me be the person to tell you, WHO GIVES A SHIT! Let them make their judgments, but if you have surrounded yourself with people that genuinely want to make a difference in their lives and share the same passions as you, show them how passionate you are and they will WANT to follow your lead.

Everyone wants to get behind someone that is passionate about their product. That product could be literally anything, something your selling, your business as a whole, your team, your group project, it doesn't matter. People will not see every hour you put into building your brand or product, but they will be able to hear the passion in your voice, and see the passion in your eyes when you have the opportunity to speak about it.

Can You Fail at Something You're Passionate About?

Just because you are passionate about something does not mean you are going to be an overnight success. There will be many trials and tribulations that you'll encounter on the way to make your passions turn into success, but because you are passionate about these things, you're willing to roll up your sleeves and do what it takes to make it work!

Being a Division 1 college soccer coach was a dream that I had since I started playing college soccer. I was fortunate enough to receive a call from a Division 1 school once I finished my Master's Degree that afforded me the opportunity to live that dream. My first few months coaching both the men and women's programs, I put everything I had in to it because I wanted to prove to everyone (including myself) that this wasn't just a passion, this was what I was meant to do. A few months go by, and I really start to settle in, and as I settle in, and in doing so I got content with going about my day and doing only the things that I knew how to do. I'd come in to the office, check to make sure the camp systems were updated, reply to any emails that needed attending to, stop by the head coach's office to make sure all alumni things were in order, prepare for that day's practice, head to practice, and then go home. Rinse and repeat. That went on for a few weeks until the top assistant coach came into the office that we shared one day and shut the door. This wasn't typical, most times when he would shut the door, it was because he was on the phone with a recruit, but it was silent. After about a minute or so of that silence, I turned around and I saw him looking at me (our desks faced opposite directions, so he was either staring at me like a creep or there was a purpose for his silence). Needless to say, there was a purpose for his silence. Before I could open my mouth to say anything to him, he asked, "What have you done to make our program better today?" So I told him the list of things that I had done which, in the moment, I felt like was a great answer. His response, "Awesome. What did you do yesterday to make our program better?" So I listed everything off again, feeling a bit less confident than with my first answer. He went on to say, "Do you think Player X is a great player?"

I said, "I think he has a lot to learn yet, but he has a ton of potential! He's right at the edge of what could be great if he just put in a bit more effort, but he will probably be a bit above average if things stay as is."

He then responds, "Yes, I definitely agree. So with where Player X is right now, do you believe that we have a whole team working toward winning a conference championship?"

I replied, "No, actually I don't. I think it'll take added effort from all of our guys to propel us to that next level. I think we're on the cusp, just not quite there."

His response to that last statement will stick with me for the rest of my life. He said, "If you can recognize that all of our team has to go above and beyond for us to get to that ELITE level, what is stopping YOU from going above and beyond to take this team to the next level?"

When you are genuinely passionate about something, and you are told that you aren't doing everything you can for that passion to succeed, it honestly feels like someone has stabbed you in the heart. I *went home that day, sat at my kitchen table and all I could think about was what I was doing, and why I wasn't doing more. Whether it was excuses I came up with in my head about how I didn't have time to do more, or how I thought I was already doing enough, I quickly realized it was all BS. The next day I wrote on a post-it note: "WHAT MORE COULD YOU BE DOING TODAY?" and stuck it on my computer monitor so that every time I had a free second, I was always contemplating new ideas for the two programs I was coaching.*

This story put a lot of things in my life into perspective. I never for a moment thought that I was 'coasting' or not giving my 100% effort. When I was working 60+ hours per week I just assumed that I was doing all that I could, but in all reality I was just working to work, I didn't really have a purpose behind what I was doing. The day this happened I promised myself that I would never again be told that I'm not doing enough because I would always try to be one, two or even three steps ahead of what I believe the 'next move' would be.

Wrap-Up (Find Your Passion)

Passion is a word that a lot of people don't truly understand. Put into words what passion and being passionate means to you. Understand the difference between the things that you like to have and the things that are priority in your life. You won't always be able to find the things that you're passionate about on your first go around, sometimes you will have to go through different trials and tribulations to find the things that you're passionate about. Don't hide your passions! Whether it is just your one true passion or multiple passions, give everyone a chance to see what it is that you care about and they will be more likely to follow you. Once you've found your passion(s), that doesn't guarantee your success, but failing doing something you're passionate about should make you more eager to learn from the mistakes that you've made and keep pushing you forward.

Chapter 8

VALUE

Identify Your Value

I genuinely believe that having the ability to identify your own value stems from seeing what value other people bring to your life and those around you. Zach Babcock, who is an entrepreneur, 'life coach', a mentor, and also a great friend of mine asked me to go work out with him one morning (I am not a morning person) when I was back visiting St. Louis. That day, for whatever reason, I made it a priority that I needed to get up and meet Zach at the Pattonville Football Field. At the time, Zach was going through a stage in his life where he was trying to do everything he could to get back in shape and live a healthy lifestyle, it just so happened that the 8 months leading up to that I was doing the exact same thing. As I pulled in to my parking space, I thought I was going there to support Zach and propel him to the next level on his journey, as I write this I am still not sure who was the greater inspiration that day. I pushed Zach to his limit for about 45 minutes doing a 60-yard sprint series and then going straight into a stadium stairs circuit. We finished, both of us exhausted, and we decided to do a few laps around the track as a cool down. The next 25 minutes changed my perspective on how to bring VALUE to another person.

Zach knew that I was looking to do more things with my life other than just coach soccer (write a book, public speaking, etc.), so he dove in and asked me questions that I never thought to ask myself. The VALUE he added to my life wasn't necessarily the questions he asked me, it was what he did next...LISTEN. The questions he asked were questions that truly made me think, which in turn, provoked me to give genuine answers. As we were finishing our second lap around the track, I realized I knew more about who I was as a person, and what I wanted to get out of my life just because of the simple method of listening. See, most people that I talk to would ask a question, hear an initial response, then weigh in on what they believed their question should have referenced, Zach didn't allow himself to do that. By Zach allowing me to understand my own logic, as silly as it may be sometimes, I realized the journey that I had started wasn't as farfetched as a majority of people in my life believed it to be.

Once I got home from the workout that day I started thinking a ton about the value I am bringing to other people. Through multiple hours of thinking, I came up with this:

Everyone brings a different type of value to every aspect of life. Value can be constituted as being great at a sport, being a great salesman because you have a certain way of talking to people, you could be a great artist, there's an insurmountable number of things that you could do to bring value. Value is oftentimes mistaken for what makes YOU successful. After that day at the track, I no longer believe that. I believe that value is how you can empower those around you so that they can help build YOU and your empire.

It's pretty crazy to think that forcing myself to get out of bed one morning to go workout with a person that I hadn't seen in years had that amount of an impact on me, but I really believe it did. Walking with Zach around the track that day made it clear to me what value he brought to people's lives. Zach's ability to ask a question that REALLY makes you think about what you want to get out of your experiences is extremely uncommon in a lot of people, and I respect the hell out of him for that because him asking me those tough questions set me on the path to success that I am on today. In the story, I mentioned, Zach's ability was not only to ask those tough questions, but also to genuinely listen.

Listening is a key attribute that everyone believes they have, but it is a skill that takes time to master. So many people think that because they have the ability to HEAR something means that they're listening; however, in essence, there is much more to it than that. Listening is analyzing, dissecting and keeping complete attention on the things that are being said. For example, if someone said to you, "Nothing in my life is going the way that I imagined it would, my family is pressuring me to get a new job because they don't think I make enough money, my girlfriend and I have been together for 3 years now, and I think she expects me to pop the question soon, and I have no idea what I'm supposed to do." I would be willing to bet that most of the people reading this right now would respond with something similar to, "Well, your parents are just looking out for you, and it has been 3 years so maybe it's time to put a ring on that finger." Is that actually helping things? Did you ACTUALLY listen to what this person is saying? Ask this person more about his job, let him talk about it, let him tell you all the things he enjoys about it, the things he may not enjoy so much, but let him talk himself into his decision. If he is unhappy enough to bring this up to you, he doesn't need another person in his life trying to make a decision for him, he needs a soundboard (someone that will listen to what he's saying without judgment) and offer rational feedback when he's done.

Obviously, the ability to listen is just one of MANY things you can do to add value to your life and to others. Value can be found in many different forms, such as, your ability to talk to people or your ability to make people feel comfortable enough to confide in you. Other attributes can be having the ability to write song lyrics better than anyone, create websites that put businesses over the top, or understand and apply accounting principles to help people with their taxes each year are all ways that you can be a valuable asset to someone, it is your job to find what your value is.

What ADDED Value Do You Bring?

When I talk about 'ADDED' value, what I mean is, what do you bring to the team that no one else has? For instance, if I'm am looking to have a website built for my new business and I've narrowed my search down to 3 people that are extremely well qualified (same degrees, same amount of experience, etc.) my next line of questioning is going to be to each of them, "What sets

IN LOVING MEMORY

Donna E. Welsch
September 9, 1950
June 25, 2018

*When I must leave you for
a little while please do not
grieve and shed wild tears
and hug your sorrow to you
through the years but start
out bravely with a gallant smile;
and for my sake and in my
name live on and do all things
the same, Feed not your loneliness
on empty days, but fill each
waking hour in useful ways,
reach out your hand in comfort
and in cheer and I in turn
will comfort you and hold
you near; and never,
never be afraid to die,
for I am waiting for
you in the sky!*

Ortmann Funeral Home
Overland, St. Louis, Missouri

you apart from everyone else?" If the first 2 people both say they can build my website exactly how I want it in 1 week and that is what they can offer me, then, the final person comes in and says I can build your website in 1 week, AND I've been working on a new format and layout structure that is extremely user friendly that I'd like to try out with you for no extra charge to receive feedback to use for future clients, I'm more likely to go with the third person because they have offered me something extra.

Added value is all about finding new ways to put yourself in a better position than your competition. Any time you have the opportunity specialize in a field or add 'another tool to your tool box' do it! Be a life-long learner, because the moment you stop learning you are falling behind the pack, and your 'added' value becomes more common.

How Do You Build Your Value?

Once you have found what value you bring to others, is that the end of the journey? Are you now a 'success'? Hell no. Now that you've found your value, it is your job to keep improving on that value. The moment you decide that you no longer need to improve yourself, is the moment that you will no longer grow as a person. Let's say your value is having the ability to speak to individuals and motivate them in whatever category they need. How do you improve on that? Put yourself in as many uncomfortable situations as possible until you become comfortable in that same situation. For example, if you are used to speaking to individuals and you've become a success doing that, make a move to speak to small groups of 5-7 and see if you have the same impact. Continue to put yourself outside of what your "comfort zone" is, do things you normally wouldn't, and do those things with confidence in yourself that you can accomplish whatever it is you set out to.

If you're uncomfortable in a situation (speaking in front of a crowd of 50+), PROJECT CONFIDENCE. It's okay to have a bit of swagger about yourself, let people see that you know what you're doing even when you're just flying by the seat of your pants. The real truth is, that is all any of us are doing. Projecting confidence is all about going into different positions and standing up for your beliefs, there's no reason not to be confident in that. In any situation, if you're projecting confidence in your voice or in the way you carry yourself, people will tend to hop on board a lot faster than if you are stumbling over your words, have nervous sweats, or just overall don't seem like you want to be involved with what's going on. At the end of the day, you have to realize that there will be one of two outcomes: you will SUCCEED or you will FAIL, how you handle the outcome will ultimately define your value and your character.

Wrap-Up (Value)

The value that you bring to a business, corporation,

team, etc. is something that is only in your control. Value can be anything from your work-ethic, your specialties, or even the way that you can relate to people. Continue to evolve yourself so you grow your ADDED VALUE. Always be willing to put yourself in situations that you wouldn't normally, to build your value. You will either succeed or you will fail, don't let that define your character.

Chapter 9

BUILD YOUR NETWORK

BE A GOOD PERSON!!

Building your network all starts with you. Are you someone that people can rely on? Are you someone that people will want to help? What are you doing for other's currently? These are questions that you must ask yourself before you can think about building your network.

As a college soccer coach, I travel all across the country working camps, meeting new people, watching women compete while playing soccer at the highest level. I've had the good fortune of being asked to sit in on 'Coach's Panels' at most every camp that I've been a part of. A coach's panel consists of 5-10 college soccer coaches sitting in front of all of the campers (usually 50-300 high school aged, female soccer players) giving advice on what it takes to be a college athlete at our respective programs. Players will ask things like, "What do you look for when you're out recruiting?", "What qualities do you look for in a player?", etc. and there will always be one consistent answer. "I look for PEOPLE that I can see myself spending 60-80 hours per week with. I'm not going to recruit someone solely on how talented they are, just so when they arrive at my school I have to be miserable coaching them for 4 years."

This fact has been relevant to me in EVERY industry that I've ever been a part of, whether it is coaching, sales, playing collegiately, or something as simple as just working on a group project. I will openly choose to separate myself from someone that I think is going to make my life more difficult because of the type of person they are. Don't get me wrong, there are definitely people out there that it will not matter what type of person they are, if they're great at what they do, the job will be theirs. I will say a great majority of business owners, managers, administration, or coaches that I am friends with have the same mentality that I have, 'Be a good person, or you won't be a part of what I'm building.'

Throughout your life, you will have thousands of people going in and out of your life, it took me a LONG time to realize that every person that I come in contact with will play a role in my life. There will be people that play a role in your everyday life, such as, a teammate, coworker, boss, girlfriend, boyfriend, husband, wife, family, etc., but there will be so many more people that play more miniscule roles in your life, such as, friend of a friend, that guy you met at Starbucks last week, the person you were walking by on the sidewalk and said "Hello!" to. Whether someone plays a large role or a smaller role in your life shouldn't matter, every role has potential to lead to something larger. For example, if I were to walk through our campus in the middle of the day and just keep my head down there's a very good chance that no one would notice who I was. On the flip side, if I walked through campus holding my head up, smiling, saying "Hello!", and maybe even asking people how they were doing, a lot more people would notice who I was. With that potentially small act, maybe I make someone's day better. Then, they tell a coworker about what happened, and decide to start supporting our team because they believe we are good people. Now, the crowds that we have at our games are growing because we have more support, which in turn, allows our team to play with more energy for our fans, which will make us a more successful program. I understand that things aren't always that simple, but expecting someone else to assume you are good person without you making a genuine effort is a lot less likely.

Are you someone that people can rely on? That's an extremely tough question to ask yourself and give an honest answer. Of course, you will most likely always feel like the answer to that is "Yes," but is it? When I think of someone that I can rely on, I always come back to 'What are you doing for others?'. Being reliable isn't always doing things when being asked to, it is also going out of your way to help people. Going out of your way for someone else could be things like donating to a cause, offering your help on a project, if you're really good at using a certain computer program (like Photoshop) teaching someone that has been having trouble marketing their business, etc. Don't get me wrong, there are so many times I have no idea how I could possibly go out of the way for some people in my life. One of the things that I like to do is randomly bring in Starbucks for my cousin (who is my team's athletic trainer). She works extremely hard for all of the girls on the team making sure they are all healthy and ready to play, so I like to go out of my way every once in a while and surprise her. The smile she has when I bring it to her is definitely worth the $4. People will always remember the little things you do for them, it may not be instantaneous, but there will be a time where you need a bit of inspiration, and those people you've helped along the way will be the first to jump on your bandwagon.

People genuinely want to help good people. It isn't

difficult and only takes a small effort to do things like smile and say "Hello!". It's our job to be good people, give people a reason to WANT to help you.

Be Around Like-Minded People

As you are in the process of building your network it is imperative that you surround yourself with people that have a similar mindset as you. If you are in the mindset that you want to constantly grind and improve yourself, don't surround yourself with people that have already gotten to a place that they are okay with where they are. Everyone has their own path, their own goals, it is our job to find people that are at similar points on their path to ensure that you aren't getting complacent. Constantly try to put yourself in the company of people who will pull you up, not those that are going to drag you down. One of the most difficult things in the world is when you realize that one of the closest friends you've had for a long time is someone that is at a different stage on their path, and you have to find a way to create some separation from that person to allow yourself to grow and become the success that you want to be.

Being connected with people that are like-minded as you, whether that is through social media, your friend group, your coworkers, your teammates, your competitors, etc. you will push yourself that much harder to not only keep up with 'the curve', but you will be pushing yourself to SET 'the curve'.

Mentors

Prideful people believe they can do everything on their own. Don't let your pride get in the way of your potential successes. Learn from other people's experiences, and make your business better because of the lessons they've learned.

In 2014, I finished grad school with a Master's Degree in Athletic Administration and I had also just finished my second year of college coaching. While coaching my college's women's soccer team, I was coaching a local high school girls' soccer team as well. The head coach of the high school team was retiring to become an assistant principal, so I thought that would be a great transitional opportunity for me while I was looking for my next college coaching opportunity. At this time, I was 24 years old, and thought I knew everything about the game of soccer...I was an idiot. I went through the interview process fully expecting that I was going to get the job, until one day I received the phone call saying they gave the job to the current boys' soccer coach of the same high school. Obviously, I was pretty upset that I didn't get offered the job, and when the coach they hired called me and asked if I wanted to stay on the girls' coaching staff, I hesitated, but then accepted the offer to be a part of the team for another year...this was one of the greatest decisions I made as a soccer coach.

A few weeks later, we had our first training session and everything I thought I knew about coaching vanished because this guy was a genius. The way he spoke to the girls, his knowledge of the game, the way he orchestrated each activity, the way he involved the rest of his staff it was like nothing I had ever seen before. After the first week of working together, I had already decided this is someone I need to emulate my coaching style around. I watched him, critically, every training session, game, player meeting, staff meeting, literally every time he spoke to someone, to try to learn from all of his prior experiences and all the knowledge he exuberated. To this day, I still believe he is one of the greatest soccer minds I have ever had the pleasure of being around.

Having this man come into my life, as unexpectedly as it happened, changed my life in such a positive way. He is now one of my greatest mentors (even though we don't talk as much as we once did), and every time I have a new 'success' in my life he is always one of my first calls because I wouldn't be the same coach...or person I am today without his mentorship. This experience put so many things in perspective for me, two things most importantly, clearly I don't know everything and I should find as many mentors as possible that I trust to build my knowledge base.

Self-Evolution is a major aspect of how we continue to find new successes within our business. Having the mindset that we know everything will halt that evolution.

The moment you think you know everything is the moment that you no longer ask questions. If you're no longer asking questions, you're no longer learning new answers, which means that you are no longer growing and evolving.

Gaining a MENTOR is the same as gaining YEARS of experience. Be willing to take advice from your mentors that have gone through the same things that you are putting yourself through right now. Most likely, the people that you'd want to be your mentor are a success or have had some sort of success throughout their careers, but they have also had their failures to get them where they are. Talk to them about their failures, learn from the things that they've done in the past so that you don't have to go through those same trenches that they've had to endure. If you are willing enough to ask a mentor for his/her advice, use that person for all the information that they are willing to give you! As they are giving you advice and telling you all of their successes and failures don't just listen in the moment, apply it to your tasks at hand. Oftentimes, information won't directly impact you where you're at in your career at the moment, but it is your job to remember it. There could be a time down the road that it may become more relevant.

Is it possible to have too many mentors? In my eyes, absolutely not! Like we said earlier, for every mentor you have, you are gaining priceless amounts of experience and knowledge. Sure, the more mentors you have the more different perspectives you may have. At the end of the day, as you're bouncing ideas off of your different mentors and receiving potentially different pieces of advice, it is your life and your decision that you have to make. Having the opportunity to hear different perspectives and different experiences could help shape your final decision as you mold those different perspectives into your new ideas. There will definitely be times that you disagree with your mentors, and that's okay! One of my greatest mentors, Trevor Banks, believed there was a job that was the right fit for me, and in the moment I didn't see it the same way. We talked through it, he gave me his ideas about why he thought it was the right fit, I talked to him about why I thought my current situation was more beneficial and eventually decided to stay where I currently was. Knowing Trevor was there for me and he and that he always wanted the best for me just made me want to push myself even harder to evolve, because I genuinely want to make him proud of the things I'm accomplishing.

Mentors can be used in many different ways, and can be utilized for more things that just accelerating your career. I would recommend having different mentors that can help advise you in every aspect of your life, whether that is in your career, relationships, family, hobbies, etc. When you start thinking about all of the different avenues in a person's life, you start to realize that it is impossible for just one person to fit the bill as a great mentor for all walks of your life. As you're making these connections in your life and finding different people that you respect enough to have them become a mentor of yours, get to know them as people. If you know their background then you will know the things that have made them successful, and the things that they may not have been as successful in.

One of the advantages of having a great mentor is that they will tell you when they think you are making a mistake. As the mentee, you have to understand that not all of the feedback you will receive from your mentors will be all butterflies and rainbows, there will be extremely tough conversations that will be had. Whether or not you agree with the feedback, take in all of the information your mentor is giving you, then you can decide whether or not you think it fits in what you're trying to accomplish.

Relating back to the story about how my boss told me that I wasn't getting my job done, even though I thought I was putting everything I had into the thing that I am passionate about; having someone tell you that all the effort and passion that you're putting into the thing that you love isn't good enough was one of the hardest realizations I've ever had. After that conversation was finished I then had two options; 1) I could sit around and bad mouth my boss for criticizing me and my work ethic because "he didn't know how much work I was putting into everything." Or 2) I could put stock in what he said, and reanalyze what my priorities were at that time in my life.

At the time, I was a 25-year old kid that loved to spend every second I could with my friends, going out drinking, playing different types of games (drinking games, video games, etc.) and that was a lot of what I looked forward to during the day. Did I NEED to spend my nights out drinking with friends? Could I have been doing more to train our players? Could I have been cutting more film for our players to watch? Could I have been watching more film to give more feedback to our players during training? Those are all questions I had to ask to give myself a perspective. Looking back, that conversation propelled me to be so much better of a coach than I thought I could have ever been. From that day forward I had a sticky note on my computer that said, "WHAT MORE CAN I DO TODAY?" I never took a minute to wait for someone to give me a task; I became EXTREMELY self-motivated, and very much adopted our team motto "TNDO" (Take No Days Off). I was so mad at my boss when he had that conversation with me, but now, I am forever grateful that he was willing to have that tough conversation with me, AND I made the decision to use the information he gave me and not just feel sorry for myself.

Wrap-Up (Build Your Network)

When you're trying to build your network, it is all going to start with you. Are you a person that people want to help and be around? Be someone people can rely on! Always try to surround yourself with like-minded people. If you're around people that are grinding and they want to be successful, that will push you to continue to grow and excel. Don't let your pride get in the way of your success! Find people that you look up to and ask them to mentor you, use their experiences to help you in the decision making processes you will have to go through in your own life. Don't hesitate to have more than one mentor, the more the merrier, and for each different avenue of your life! Mentors are not just all butterflies and rainbows, be willing to take criticism and use the advice they are giving you, and make it beneficial to what you're trying to build. Surround yourself with people that are constantly pulling you to a higher place, not those that are going to drag you down, and slow down the progress of your career.

Chapter 10

GOAL SETTING: ROAD TRIP METHOD

My goal setting method, The Road Trip Method, is something that I came up with a few years ago, and is something that I use in multiple aspects of my life all the time. I came up with this method actually on a road trip from Springfield, Missouri to St. Louis, Missouri. The trip from Springfield to St. Louis is a little over 200 miles all on one highway, it is not a fun drive. I started thinking about ways that I could make the trip seem like it was going by faster, so I broke the trip down in to three different 'CHECKPOINTS'. Each checkpoint was between 50-60 miles from the next, so instead of having one long trip of 200+ miles, I have four shorter trips of 50-60 miles, and that was just easier for me to wrap my head around.

Once I came up with the checkpoints, I started thinking a bit more about what I really wanted to get out of this trip. When I get to St. Louis (FINAL DESTINATION), what are the things that I plan to do? Get in my best friend's hot tub? – Of course. Are we going to go golfing? – Good chance. Will we go out to dinner with some friends and family? – Most likely. Now that I knew the different things I wanted to do once I got to St. Louis, I could start planning the things I need to prepare before I leave Springfield (INITIAL PREPARATION). I would definitely need to bring my golf clubs, some clothes to go to dinner, and then a pair of swim trunks to get in the hot tub. I know I'll also need to get gas, check my tire pressure and get an oil change to make sure we can make it all the way to St. Louis.

As I started to think about all this stuff in my car, it hit me, I can use this exact way of thinking to start setting goals! I would first come up with my long-term goal (Final Destination), build in 3 short-term goals that allow me a timeline and reference points to make it seem more attainable (Checkpoints), and finally prepare myself with whatever it is that I need to get started on the right path (Initial Preparation).

Allow Your Goals to Connect Your Values

When you are in the process of setting your goals, always allow the goals that you are setting in place to connect with the values that are important to you. All of the different beliefs and values that we've talked about leading up to this moment should be a point of emphasis while you are cataloging your 'Road Trip'.

Initial Preparation

In the stage of Initial Preparation, it is important to understand what your equivalent to "gassing up, getting an oil change, or putting air in the tires" would be. At this stage, you need to figure out what your WHY is. Why do you want to get to the destination that you've chosen? How is this 'Road Trip' going to impact your life?

The Initial Preparation stage is also used to understand the different avenues of your life, and how each will be impacted by the journey that you are planning. The common 'avenues' of life would be Personal, Professional, and Relationship. Obviously, there are more avenues that you could add to this, but I've added these three to each of my Road Trips. It is extremely important to find a balance between the different avenues in this stage or else as you begin to plan the rest of this trip things will remain unbalanced, and things in your life will receive less attention than they deserve. Each of these avenues do not have to have the same timetables. For instance, your next professional 'road trip' may be a 6-month project, whereas, there may be something in your personal life that you want to work on for the next 12 months. As long as you know, and understand, that each of your goals have different checkpoints and timelines, that is what really matters.

As you gain experience (another way of saying 'getting older'), you realize that you can't change everything in your life in an instant. It works the same way when you are setting your goals. Aim high with your destination, but be sure to keep your checkpoints realistic. You should be setting your final destination so high that people question you, like, "Do you actually think you can do that?" 'Hell yes you can!' Setting a goal and aiming high is one thing, but YOU have to believe that you can do it. Trust the process that you are going to create; Trust that the checkpoints that you set will lead you to where you want to go. With a lofty final destination, you have to put a ton of thought in to putting the correct checkpoints into place along the way. Each checkpoint should be something that is attainable. Then, within each checkpoint should be a step-by-step breakdown of what you can/need to do to reach that next checkpoint. Taking your trip one checkpoint at a time and trusting your process will lead you to the success that you're looking for.

The last piece of advice for your Initial Preparation is to WRITE THINGS DOWN. Don't just think about your goals; Write them down so you have something that you can reference back to when you are feeling concerned about your progress. All throughout school we would be handed these day planners, it was basically a calendar that allowed you to write down notes and schedule when you had upcoming tests, quizzes or things like that, I literally never used them. I used to be an idiot. I was always flying by the seat of my pants hoping that I would remember the things I needed to study or making sure I completed all of the homework that I was meant to have finished on time. That's just not a good way to live, I was literally setting myself up for failure time and time again. Don't allow yourself to guess what your goals are. Having this 'road trip' means literally nothing if you can't remember where you're going. Remember to stay on course once you've gotten everything written down. You've got these goals and checkpoints written down for a reason, if you are straying off-course, revisit your checkpoints to allow yourself to get back on track.

Checkpoint 1

Checkpoint 1 is the first of your short term milestones that will lead you to your final destination. This checkpoint should represent approximately 25% of the overall project that you are working on. Checkpoint 1 is most times the most difficult to complete because a ton of people forget or don't care to do things in the Initial Preparation stage. So many people think they don't need to write things down (I used to be one of these people), and they forget some of their best ideas. They decide to aim smaller because they aren't seeing that instant success that we talked about earlier. People will not completely map out steps to get to a realistic checkpoint. Finally, people will tie all of the avenues in their lives together which will lead to having a lack of focus on the task or tasks at hand.

I highly recommend putting a timeline on each checkpoint as well as a percentage of completion. For example, if you want to finish your total project in a 4-month timeframe, (Assuming your start date is June 1) I would write something to the effect of "Checkpoint 1: Due before July 1". By having this timeframe, it forces you to keep up with your tasks and it is another way to hold yourself accountable when no one else is looking.

Checkpoint 2

Checkpoint 2 is the half-way mark of your trip. Around 50% of your overall project should be complete up to this point. At this point in your process things should start to resemble what your final project should end up looking like. For example, if you're writing a book, by your Checkpoint 2 you should already have completed your entire outline, now you know the flow of the material, and now leading into Checkpoint 3 you are starting to put those ideas in your outline into words. Your goal, at this point, is to make sure you finish, and clean up enough of your chapters in time for editing and publishing by your deadline date.

As you are planning a timetable for Checkpoint 2, you want to keep your timeline for Checkpoint 2 similar to that of Checkpoint 1 (ie. Checkpoint 1 – 1 month; Checkpoint 2 – 1 month). I like the idea of keeping these timeframes the same because it allows you to have a similar schedule and rhythm through the entirety of your 'trip'.

Checkpoint 3

As you get to Checkpoint 3, you've now reached the 75% mark for your trip, and things are starting to get real.

At this stage, you should just be polishing everything off or securing any loose ends that you may have been waiting on. For example, (we'll use the writing a book example again) you will now be sending your book to your editor, doing any revisions that may be necessary, and working on the finalization of publishing your book.

The most important step in the process once you've reached Checkpoint 3 is to make sure you are not rushing the final project. In this step, be extremely crucial about all of the small details. Don't rush things because you are close to being finished. So many times, when you are "in the homestretch", people tend to forget about the little details as their only thoughts become about just wanting to finish. Keep your eye on the small details, at this point you've put in months of work, you don't want to start getting sloppy the last few weeks and ruin all of the hard work and preparation you put into the rest of this project. Allowing yourself to stay focused on every detail will permit you take your project from something that people will see as well done, to something that people will see as instrumental in the development of their career.

Final Destination

THIS IS IT. This is the end goal for your trip. To continue with our writing a book example, the final destination for your book would be your publication date. The date that you set for your final destination will typically be the first date that you set. So, going back to the previous example that we talked about during Checkpoint 1 (again assuming that we start on June 1), if we wanted to set a 4-month timeframe I would set my 'Publish Date' as October 1. So the rest of the timetable would be as follows:

- Initial Preparation: June 1
- Checkpoint 1: July 1
- Checkpoint 2: August 1
- Checkpoint 3: September 1

- <u>Final Destination:</u> October 1

Now that you're here, what is it that you want to get out of this trip? No one ever just plans a trip to go somewhere, finally make it, and then just turn around and leave, just so they can then look back on it and say, "Hey! I went there!" A great example of this would be your family wants to take a road trip to Orlando from St. Louis, and you all plan out everything that it is going to take for you to get there, what snacks you're going to need, where you want to stop to eat, where you need to stop to get gas, maybe you need to stop and stay the night in a hotel on the way since it is a 14-hour drive, EVERYTHING is planned. Eventually, you and your family reach Orlando, is that ENOUGH for you? Hell NO! You will want to experience as much as you can once you've reached Orlando, go to Disney World, Universal Studios, Sea World, all of the attractions!

Every detail that you want to accomplish in this step is EXTREMELY important! If you fly by the seat of your pants in this step, all of your preparation in getting here will all seem wasted. It may be great, and turn out well for one 'Road Trip', but then you think that by everything working out once that way, and now you start taking shortcuts, you start to lose your dedication to your preparation, which will in time hinder your success. Don't allow yourself to put in all of that work, and fall into the trap of chasing the instant gratification.

Now that you've reached the final destination, you can relax and start taking things easy, right? Since you've reached the final destination that you set months ago, that makes you a 'success', right? No!! You reaching the final destination for this trip is definitely a success, but it is not something that will define you as successful. Now that you've gotten to this point, reflect back on the journey that you had, because now, it is time to start a new 'Road Trip', and the FINAL DESTINATION that you've just reached is now your INITIAL PREPARATION. Be proud of yourself, you worked extremely hard to get to where you are, but don't let one success define you. Your next 'Road Trip' is waiting for you!

Wrap-Up (Goal Setting: Road Trip Method)

Goal setting, in my opinion, should be a main priority in everyone's life. All of the values and attributes mentioned throughout this book should tie in to your goals and the way that you achieve them. In my goal setting method, Road Trip Method, the first thing you should coordinate is what your Final Destination is. It doesn't make sense to start planning something without know where you're going first.

Once you've decided your Final Destination, develop a timeline that you want your project to be completed in. Your Initial Preparation stage should include the date you plan to start your project as well as the different things that you will need to complete before you start your trip leading into Checkpoint 1. For the 3 separate Checkpoints, try to have a consistent timeframe to work with each of them that correlates with the timeline that you have set with your Final Destination. Each

Checkpoint should have detailed 'short-term' goals that are realistic and attainable. Along with these goals should be details of how you could potentially reach these goals and continue your project in the right direction.

When you're setting your Final Destination, reach for the stars every time you have to set a new one. Make people think that you are crazy for how high you are setting your goals. Trust the process, and prove them wrong.

ACKNOWLEDGMENTS

There are so many people in my life that have molded me in to the person that I am today. There's no way I could even begin to name everyone, but I'll try my best.

First to my mom, thank you for always wanting me to push the envelope. Thank you for having bigger dreams for me than I could have ever imagined, without you pushing me at a young age I would've never been confident enough to force myself in to situations that I wasn't' comfortable in. You are my greatest motivation, and I live my life to make you proud, I hope I'm doing a good job so far.

ROAD TRIP TO SUCCESS

To my dad, Thank you for being a great role model. You are a prime example of what it means to be a great person. Even when times get tough, you're positive, you're encouraging, you're non-judgmental, and I know you always have my back. I've said my mom is my greatest motivation, but you are the person that I aspire to be. Battling through cancer showed your strength and courage, but the way you seem to battle and push through every obstacle that is thrown at you in life is what I truly admire. Thank you for everything.

To my grandma, thank you for always putting others before yourself, and teaching me that the best things in life are shared through others. You have always been my biggest fan and there's no way I would be where I am today without you!

To my brother and sister, thank you for always finding a way to support me. We haven't always been on the same paths, but you both have always found a way to support me. I am the person I am today because of how hard we pushed each other.

To all of my amazing friends, whether I grew up with you, known you for 15 years, started out as friends through other friends, or moved to your city and you took me in as one of your own I have been extremely blessed with the great people that are in my life. Thank you, all of you, for the countless laughs, the mentorship, the places to stay when I come back to visit your cities ☺, and thank you all so much for pushing yourselves to be successful. There's a chapter in this book about surrounding yourself with people that pull you up, not drag you down...I've been extremely lucky to be around people that want to succeed my whole life, because of your examples I've always wanted to continue to grow. A special thank you to the Smith family. Pete, Nick, Lauren, Janet, Dave (and all cousins, aunts, uncles, etc.), you all have welcomed me as a family member since I can remember. I will be forever grateful for all that you've done for me, thank you!

To all of teammates and coaches that I've had throughout my career, you all have taught me what it really means to work hard, manage my time, and do things for something that is larger than myself. Through the sleepless nights, grueling practices, great wins, and agonizing defeats I have gained brothers for life, and I will never forget everything that each of you have done for me throughout my career.

Finally, to all of the players that I've had the pleasure to coach, thank you for pushing me every day to better myself for you. I will forever be a student of the game of soccer and of life, through your questions, commitment, and drive I have continuously had to find new ways to better myself. In my time as a coach, I have found that a mutual respect between coach and player produces the greatest results. I've been extremely fortunate with the many teams that I've coached. The respect that I've received from my players has led to many great, life-long friendships that I will forever be grateful for.

ROAD TRIP TO SUCCESS

THANK YOU

I have 3 massive THANK YOU's to hand out. First, to STACIE MASSEY and the rest of the Massey family for taking the time to edit this book. This being my first book, I had no idea what to expect, and Stacie worked diligently to get this done, THANK YOU!

Next, to MAY PHAN for putting my cover together. Again, this being my first book, she helped explain the process to me, went above and beyond every time I asked her to edit or change something, and everything was always done way faster than I could have expected, THANK YOU!

Finally, to MARY DISIDORE for writing such a well-thought out Foreword. Mary was a player of mine at Missouri State, and she ALWAYS put her passion and pride in to everything she did, much like she did in her piece in this book. I am honored that you were willing to put yourself out there and tell a bit of your story in my first book. THANK YOU!